APPALOOSAS

by Victor Gentle and Janet Perry

Gareth Stevens Publishing
MILWAUKEE

For a free color catalog describing Gareth Stevens' list of high-quality books and multimedia programs, call 1-800-542-2595 (USA) or 1-800-461-9120 (Canada). Gareth Stevens Publishing's Fax: (414) 225-0377. See our catalog, too, on the World Wide Web: gsinc.com

Library of Congress Cataloging-in-Publication Data

Gentle, Victor.
   Appaloosas / by Victor Gentle and Janet Perry.
      p.   cm. — (Great American horses: an imagination library series)
   Includes bibliographical references (p. 23) and index.
   Summary: Describes the history and characteristics that distinguish these horses from other breeds.
      ISBN 0-8368-2129-7 (lib. bdg.)
      1. Appaloosa horse—Juvenile literature. [1. Appaloosa horse. 2. Horses.]
   I. Perry, Janet, 1960- . II. Title. III. Series: Gentle, Victor. Great American horses.
   SF293.A7G443   1998
   636.1'3—dc21   98-14797

First published in 1998 by
Gareth Stevens Publishing
1555 North RiverCenter Drive, Suite 201
Milwaukee, WI 53212 USA

Text: Victor Gentle and Janet Perry
Page layout: Victor Gentle, Janet Perry, and Renee M. Bach
Cover design: Renee M. Bach
Series editor: Patricia Lantier-Sampon
Editorial assistants: Mary Dykstra and Diane Laska

Photo credits: Cover, pp. 5, 7, 9, 11, 13, 15, 17, 19, 21, and 22 © Bob Langrish.

Printed in the United States of America

1 2 3 4 5 6 7 8 9 02 01 00 99 98

Front cover: An Appaloosa with roan and red spots, like this one, might be hard to see on a snow-covered hill. Nature guards it by scattering spots on its coat.

TABLE OF CONTENTS

Words that appear in the glossary are printed in **boldface** type the first time they occur in the text.

OLD WORLD HORSES, NEW WORLD BREED

When Europeans first came to the New World in the late fifteenth century, American Indians were amazed by what they saw. The European explorers seemed very tall and were able to move very fast. In fact, it appeared they had two heads and six legs — until the Europeans got off their high horses!

When the American Indians saw the horses and what they could do, the Indians wanted them, too. They traded items and food for horses, kidnapped them, and captured **Mustangs** (horses that had escaped and lived in the wild). Soon, they rode better than the Europeans. Next, they **bred** better horses. Horses were the best things the Europeans could own, trade, or give away.

Field friends snuggling on a cold day. The Tennessee Walking Horse seems to prefer a spotted pillow of just the right height.

THE "GOOD MEDICINE" HORSE

The Nez Percé Indians believed that people who left for dangerous adventures should paint their bodies to be safe from angry spirits. The Indians called this "making good medicine."

The Nez Percé also believed that spotted horses were born with good medicine, because they were painted by nature. After all, if your horse was not guarded from evil spirits, how could you be safe?

So, the Indians bred spotted horses that worked hard with little food. To do this, the Indians carefully picked mares (female horses) and stallions (male horses) to **mate** and give birth to foals (baby horses) that were spotted and especially strong.

Nature has wrapped this foal in a white baby blanket and scattered its mother's back with dots like the flowers in their meadow.

NAME THAT HORSE!

When the new Americans from Europe explored the West, they reported that the Nez Percé's brightly patterned horses were sure-footed, strong, healthy, and easy to train. These horses were exceptional!

So, they were given a name all their own. First, the horses were named *Palouse Horses*, because they lived near the Palouse River in the Pacific Northwest region of America. That changed to *A Palousy Horse*, then *Appaloosy*, and, finally, *Appaloosa*.

A good horse is easy to find all over the United States. The Appaloosa on the left sports leopard spots. The one on the right is a strawberry **roan**.

THE HORSE UNDER THE SPOTS

Appaloosas have special features in addition to their spots. Appaloosa eyes have a **sclera,** which is a ring of white around the colored area (the **iris** and the **pupil**). The American Indians thought this made the horses look human.

Their hooves have black-and-white, up-and-down stripes. The hooves are so hard the horses do not need shoes. Around the mouth and between their back legs, the skin is **parti-colored**, which sounds like the Appaloosas are ready for fun! "Parti-colored" means the skin is colored in parts. In fact, this skin is pink with dark spots.

Finally, Appaloosas' manes and tails are called **rattails** because there is very little hair there.

Look closely at the face of the Appaloosa standing in front. Can you see the sclera, the parti-coloring on its mouth, and the thin hair in its forelock?

SPOTS THAT DISAPPEAR BEFORE YOUR EYES

Horses have had spots since their beginning. The earliest kind of prehistoric horse, which scientists named *eohippus*, or the *Dawn Horse*, had stripes and spots on its fur. The patterns made it easy for the horses to hide from predators (animals that eat other animals).

Yet, Appaloosa spots are tricky. Sometimes, an Appaloosa foal is born roan (white hair mixed in evenly over a darker coat). Then, as it gets older, it may grow white areas over its hips and withers. Breeders know that the pattern of each Appaloosa coat can be quite a surprise.

These two foals are having a little bit of fun. Although mostly red as a foal, the roan may grow whiter as it gets older.

BRIGHT SPOTS, DARK SPOTS, NO SPOTS

An Appaloosa's coat can have at least five different patterns, listed below. Some Appaloosa horses have coats that combine patterns.

1. *Blanket:* The horse has a solid color from its head to its ribs and over the front and back legs. The rear is white. The horse may have big spots, little spots, or no spots.

2. *Frost:* The horse has a solid-colored body, with white specks all over it, like a starry sky.

3. *Leopard:* The horse has a white body, with dark spots all over, like a Dalmatian dog.

4. *Marble:* The horse is roan on its face, neck, and lower legs. The rest of its body is frosted, or has lots of little white spots all over.

5. *Snowflake:* The horse has a solid color over most of the body with white spots over the rear end.

Match each horse's pattern to the descriptions above. Are there any leopard patterns in this group?

HOW THE SPOTS WERE NEARLY WIPED OUT

After the American Civil War, settlers moving West battled with Indians over land. The Nez Percé did not want to be confined to reservations, so some escaped on their Appaloosas. Eventually, all the Nez Percé were captured. Chief Joseph, their leader, promised that the Nez Percé would never run or fight the U.S. Army again. But the officer in charge was sure the Nez Percé would escape if they were allowed to keep their horses.

He ordered the soldiers to run the Appaloosas off a cliff, but the horses still had a little "good medicine" left. The soldiers knew it was foolish to kill such good horses. They kept the best Appaloosas and saved the **breed** from extinction.

A captive audience of lucky descendants of the Nez Percé's Appaloosas. Can you tell which one is a snowflake, and which is a frost?

THE KEEPER OF THE SPOTS

In 1937, Claude Thompson, from Oregon, was shocked by a news article about the Appaloosas. Only a few hundred horses remained, he learned. Once, there had been many thousands.

He worried that no one was breeding Appaloosas as carefully as the Nez Percé had. True, without the soldiers who had rescued the horses from the Army, not even these few hundred would be alive. Without good breeding control, however, the Appaloosa breed would still be lost.

Thompson set up a list of features that indicate a true Appaloosa. Other breeders agreed to honor the list and to breed for those features. In this way, the Appaloosas were saved.

At Appaloosa horse shows, a very popular event is the Costume Class that honors the Nez Percé. Although these people aren't Nez Percé, they have the spirit!

WHAT SPOTS APPALOOSAS FILL

An Appaloosa's parents may be Quarter Horses, Morgans, Saddlebreds, Thoroughbreds, or Arabians. As long as the foal grows up to have the right markings, it is an Appaloosa. With all these different breeds in their backgrounds, Appaloosas can do many kinds of work.

Some Appaloosas help people who live with disabilities learn to ride. An Appaloosa named Spot was one of these horses. As he got older, Spot needed special care, which his owner, John Castle, happily provided. After all, Spot had helped a lot of people for many years.

The Appaloosas' work is as varied as their coat patterns. They are always ready to do the job.

How many coat patterns can you find on this Appaloosa? This one "turns its hoof" nicely to pulling an English carriage called a phaeton.

DIAGRAM AND SCALE OF A HORSE

Here's how to measure a horse with a show of hands.
This ideal Appaloosa has several patterns on its coat.

6 ft. (180 cm)	18 hh
5 ft. (150 cm)	17 hh
	16 hh
	15 hh
	14 hh
4 ft. (120 cm)	13 hh
	12 hh
	11 hh
3 ft. (90 cm)	10 hh
	9 hh
	8 hh
2 ft. (60 cm)	7 hh
	6 hh
	5 hh
1 ft. (30 cm)	4 hh
	3 hh
	2 hh
	1 hand

(10-year-old)

1 hand high (hh) = 4 inches (approximately 10 cm)

WHERE TO WRITE OR CALL FOR MORE INFORMATION

Appaloosa Horse Club
5070 Highway 8 West
Moscow, ID 83843
Phone: (208) 882-5578

22

MORE TO READ AND VIEW

Books (Nonfiction):   *The Complete Guides to Horses and Ponies* (series). Jackie Budd
(Gareth Stevens)
A Day in the Life of a Horse Trainer. Charlotte McGuinn Freeman
(Troll Associates)
Great American Horses (series). Victor Gentle and Janet Perry
(Gareth Stevens)
Magnificent Horses of the World (series). Tomáš Míček and
Dr. Hans-Jörg Schrenk (Gareth Stevens)
Wild Horse Magic for Kids. Animal Magic (series). Mark Henckel
(Gareth Stevens)
Wild Horses of the Red Desert. Glen Rounds (Holiday House)

Books (Fiction):   *Herds of Thunder, Manes of Gold.* Edited by B. Coville (Doubleday)
Jodie's Journey. Colin Theile (Harper & Row)
Saddle Club (series). Bonnie Bryant (Gareth Stevens)
Wild Appaloosa. Glen Rounds (Holiday House)

Videos (Fiction):   *The Black Stallion.* (MGM Home Video)
Run, Appaloosa, Run. (Walt Disney)

WEB SITES

About Appaloosas: Appaloosa Horse Club:
www.appaloosa.com/youth.htm
www.bcm.nt

For interactive games:
www.haynet.net/kidstuff.html

For general horse information:
www.haynet.net
www.ladyhawk.mcn.net
okstate.edu/breeds/horses

Due to the dynamic nature of the Internet, some web sites stay current longer than others.
To find additional web sites, use a reliable search engine with one or more of the following
keywords to help you locate information about horses: *Arabians, equitation, Morgans,
Mustangs, Nez Percé, racing,* and *Thoroughbreds.*

GLOSSARY

You can find these words on the pages listed. Reading a word in a sentence helps you understand it even better.

breed (n) — a group of horses that share the same features as a result of the careful selection of stallions and mares to mate 16, 18, 20

breed (v), **bred** — to choose a stallion and a mare with certain features to make foals with similar features 4, 6, 18

iris (EYE-ris) — the colored part of the eye 10

mate (v) — to join (animals) together to produce young; to breed a male and a female 6

Mustangs — wild American horses 4

parti-colored — skin that is pink with dark spots 10

pupil (PYU-pl) — the black center of the eye 10

rattails — tails and manes with very little hair 10

roan — having white or other light hairs over a darker coat color, such as red, brown, or black. For example, a strawberry roan has a dark red coat with white or another light-colored hair 8, 9, 12, 13, 14

sclera (SKLAIR-uh) — a white ring around the iris of an eye 10

INDEX